TRAGEDY
to TRIUMPH

TESTIMONIES OF TRAUMA AND SPIRITUAL GROWTH

Dr. Fatima A. McCoy-Leonard

Book Cover Design: Prize Publishing House
Photography By: Annette Jones

Printed by: Prize Publishing House, LLC in the United States of America.

First printing edition 2023.

Prize Publishing House
P.O. Box 9856, Chesapeake, VA 23321
www.PrizePublishingHouse.com

Library of Congress Control Number: 2023910237

ISBN (Paperback): 979-8-9884324-0-1
ISBN (E-Book): 979-8-9884324-1-8

Pain, Sorrow, and Spiritual Healing

Testimonies of Trauma and Journey to Spiritual Healing
to Inspire You to Persevere Through Your Circumstances

I challenge you to take one step forward at a
time, eventually releasing altogether.

Contents

Dedication

I dedicate this book to God's children who are struggling to move past their trauma and seeking direction. Perhaps you want redemption and do not know the steps to take or how to develop a relationship with God. After reading my testimonies, I pray that you will be strengthened through Christ to overcome your past trauma that may seem paralyzing.

Foreword

I am humbled as this author's Pastor and Spiritual Shepherd for nearly a decade to pen this message! I am honored to bless this impressive and impactful body of work!

The ills of our society have eroded our confidence in institutions of family, community, and faith-based organizations that have established our healthy being! The complexity and vicissitudes of this generation and those we are privileged to serve must be addressed effectively to obtain any relevance of solace. Whatever our chosen professions, careers, vocations, and pre-wired assignments, there are multilayered challenges, especially post-pandemic!

There is a void of authentic, organic, and transparent commentary on the deep-seated, often suppressed emotions of the residue of childhood and family trauma! An author of this caliber emerges with timely insights into areas of our fractured systems that we desire to disappear!

Courageously Dr. McCoy-Leonard shines a light on the crevices of her childhood trauma and its effects on our emotional stability and well-being. She details through systematic work how she overcomes and invites her readers to prescriptively to the same.

Her insight from years of dedicated work highlights how critical awareness is essential to developing holistic wellness. As stakeholders charged with creating a healthy space for our individual and collective potential future genius being cultivated!

This book details and describes some deep areas of productive examination to empower the reader for purposeful execution. She gleans from her varied experiences to candidly share through literature, scripture, and music in an antidotal way, not to ignore or dismiss the event but to process it in a way that makes it more beneficial and less obstructive.

It is sheer cathartic work as Dr. McCoy-Leonard chronicles episodes and meaningful events she has lived through and defines techniques for thriving through them, not just surviving them. It has been my learned experience that when trauma is "faced," internalizing its impact applying principles that evoke change and transformation, one is genuinely better, not bitter. It is a tremendous blessing to endorse this project, and I look forward to all that will proceed due to her diligence. It is hopeful and helpful to those who will follow the path toward transformative lives!

A true must-read and share!

Pastor Lola A. Baker, B.A., MPA, MAR

Preface

My name is Dr. Fatima A. McCoy-Leonard. I am a servant of God, a doctor of educational leadership, and I love empowering others to see their greatness.

The Holy Spirit led me to write this book. Throughout my life, I have encountered people struggling to move past their traumatic experiences. Some people make a conscious effort, while others become stagnant. In my attempt to empower them to let go and move forward, they have come up with many reasons why it is impossible. I would say *if only you knew what I have been through*. I do not look like what I have been through, but through God's grace and mercy, I have come out of it; yet I have never shared my life's experiences.

I pray that after reading my book, you will desire to improve some aspects of your life. Maybe you need a way out of your unfavorable circumstances. We are all a work in progress, striving for perfection. Yet, we do not realize how much we need God. I learned I could not get there without keeping God at the forefront of my life.

This book depicts my childhood experiences with trauma and how my spirituality helped me overcome life's struggles to live victoriously. I will give you a glimpse into my childhood and the complex trauma I experienced, followed by my path to spiritual awakening and growth, all of which played a role in cultivating the person I am.

Each chapter contains scripture, prayer, and songs that have inspired and helped me along my journey. Music has always been inspirational, and I use it as motivation to propel me forward. Perhaps you will find it helpful.

First, please reflect on your purpose for reading my testimonies. Throughout this book, I will ask thought-provoking questions so that you may self-reflect and develop profound awareness of your strengths. What would you like to glean from my experiences? Are you looking for self-awareness? Improved relationships? Are you looking to grow in Christ? Renewed Faith? I ask that you read intently and pray that my testimonies help you overcome imposter syndrome, fear, anxiety, or any obstacles that impede you from living the life God has designed for you.

At the hem of your family may lie life-long secrets, feuds, and generational trauma. This trauma can either help or stunt your growth. You need to work through your trauma and release it. They say generational curses are unreal, and I did not believe it, as my family has endured generations of trauma and dysfunction. I can testify that I have broken them if there is such a thing as generational curses.

Trauma is not a new phenomenon. I have endured trauma since childhood; yet, growing up, I did not identify my experiences as traumatic; it seemed normal but not ideal. Nevertheless, in my early adulthood, I realized I did not have to stay stuck in it. This is my story and the tools I have gained and continue to employ to elevate past my trauma.

Trauma comes in many forms and at various times. Some circumstances sometimes exist outside of your control. Sometimes there is no warning to prepare you for how to respond. It just appears and slaps you in the face, and in the moment, you react or respond and pray for the best outcome. This seemed to be constant during my youth. I have experienced multiple traumatic experiences, sometimes simultaneously.

Undoubtedly, you must know that your past trauma does not have to define who you are. Your ability to persevere through your trauma is a testament to your strength. It is not about what you have been through but, more importantly, how you grow through those experiences.

You are the determining factor of your progression or whether you remain in the past. I am not saying you have to forget your experience; however, ignoring or burying your trauma may result in the trauma resurfacing or manifesting into anger, resentment, and despair. Give yourself the grace to process and grow through the pain.

Foundationally, growing up, I was implicitly or explicitly told to hold on to family secrets. In the words of my grandmother, my father's mother, "What goes on in this house stays in this house," and "Don't air your dirty laundry in the streets." Naturally, I held on to that mindset most of my life, making writing this book a bit difficult. Yet it is liberating to share my whole story without fear of judgment or criticism. To some extent, I was protecting my family from scrutiny. Now, I am ready to reveal my multiple layers of trauma through my complex story.

Whereas talking about traumatic experiences repeatedly and reliving the difficult trials may be emotionally overwhelming, it has been therapeutic for me; however, decades later, the pain of the past traumatic experiences continues to adversely affect my family. My pastor always reminds the congregation that what the devil meant for harm, God meant for good. I am blessed to share my testimonials.

My story may not be your story, but there may be something that you need support getting through. I pray that you will be inspired to overcome obstacles and live abundantly. I warn you that I do not want sympathy or pity. I desire for you to do the work to become a better you.

Remember, God is love.

<u>Song of Inspiration</u>

"My Testimony" ~ Marvin Sapp

Acknowledgments

Thank God for giving me the words to put on the pages, the knowledge, and the understanding to grow through every lived experience. Otherwise, this book would not exist.

To my husband, Chris, who always encourages me to do God's work. When I sleep a little later on Saturday morning, you always say, "You're not out saving the world today." You always reassure me that I am great and you are not surprised by my accomplishments. Instead, you would be surprised if I did not accomplish a goal.

To my sister, Shakura, God has brought us through. Thank you for being the source of strength I needed to navigate my childhood. You always had my back and fought for me when necessary. I do not know where I would be without you. You are stronger than you know and will have insurmountable success. Keep conquering your goals.

To my sister, Yasmin, you have selflessly shared your mother with me since our childhood. We became sisters the moment my father and your mother locked eyes. Mommy Wanda definitely came at a time I needed a motherly figure. Thank you for your continued support and for having my back. You keep me inspired through encouraging words and wisdom.

My sisters in Christ, Linda McCrary and future doctor Lashaun Daniels-Edney, thank you for the prayers, tears, and motivational and spiritual talks. We all need sisters who love us unconditionally and those we can rely on. You have been that for me.

Mia, we all need someone we can connect with on a girlfriend level, "Who gets us." God placed you in my life when I did not know I needed you. We have kept each other inspired and have gone through high school, college, and our careers together and continue to prosper. Although I have not been able to bear children, God allowed you to bless me to become a parent. Thanks for my godson.

My friends, Saleemah and Chauntay, we have been friends since high school, and I am grateful that God has blessed us with decades of friendship. Thanks for your loyalty and encouragement.

Pastors John and Lula Baker, thank you for accepting me into your congregation to fellowship with the C4 family. I appreciate your ongoing prayers, guidance, and blessings. Thank you for always showing up when I need you.

Thank you to my father, Stanley Boyd. You are the first intelligent man I met as a child. You were my superhero and always held me on your shoulders so that I could touch the sky. At least, that is what it felt like as a child. Thank you for believing in me and giving me sound advice. You are my first love!

Aunt Jeanette, thank you for staying connected with me during those crucial years of my life. For that, I got to build connections with our family.

Thank you to all my family, friends, and brothers and sisters in Christ who have kept me in your prayers and given me encouraging words and pep talks throughout my journey.

Soror Annette Jones, thank you for the amazing photography. You are truly Godsent.

Lastly, my guardian angel, my mother, whom I have not had the opportunity to call mom since I was about three or four years old, Laverne (Aminah) McCoy. Somehow, I always felt your spirit around me and your comforting hands holding me. I love you. ~ Be blessed!

Tragedy

My reality…

It was my junior year of high school. Months before my sister's senior prom, I witnessed, during that time, the most traumatic event of my life. Nothing could have prepared me for what was about to transpire.

She pierced the knife at her neck as she approached me.
"I'm going to kill myself. Tima, I don't want to live anymore."
I shouted, "What's wrong with you, Kim?! Put the knife down, Kim! Kim, pleeeease," I cried and pleaded, "Put the knife down! Don't do that to yourself; what's wrong?!"
"Look," she said to me, then slashed her neck.
"Oh my God, Kim, What's wrong?!" I shouted again.
Blood gushed from her neck.

I ran to get help from the next-door neighbors. **Bang, Bang, Bang!**

"Open the door! Help!!! My sister, I don't know what's wrong with my sister!!!! Please help! Call the Ambulance! She cut herself!!!!"

When I turned around, she sliced her wrist. I could hear the neighbors race to the door. I could hear talking in the background. They had strong Haitian accents, but I could understand. We always had a good rapport with them. We sometimes looked after their younger daughter when they were preoccupied with work. I knew I could count on them for help.

"What is it? What's wrong?"
"Oh, my God! Hurry, call the ambulance!"
Before I could get back to her, she had already done it. She jumped!
She jumped out the two-story window. *She'll never survive,* I thought.
I screamed, "My sister!!!!! Please help her. I don't know what's wrong with her."

I quickly called my grandmother Hattie, but her ride to the house was seemingly long. It was not that she did not want to be there, but she lived about 40 minutes away.

"She did what?!?! Awww! God dammit! What the hell is wrong with Kim?! She always gives me problems. I'll be there, Tima; let me call Sandy to come to the house."

My grandmother called my aunt, who only lived about 15 minutes away, to meet the police and ambulance at the house. I was a minor, so I could not accompany my sister to the hospital.

Since my aunt, Sandy, was closer in proximity than my grandmother, she had a better chance of making it to us before my grandmother arrived. She made it to our place just as the ambulance arrived. It was late at night and dark outside, so there were not many people outside to witness the traumatic event.

The ambulance finally rushed my sister to the hospital. Suddenly, everything went blank for her and me. This was the first time in my life I felt alone.

Confused and Scared

At this moment, I realized I needed God more than I thought and greater than I knew.

This was certainly not the beginning of my trauma.

Scripture

"The Lord is on my side; I will not fear: what can man do unto me?" ~ Psalm 118:6

"Now faith is the substance of things hoped for, the evidence of things not seen." ~ Hebrews 11:1

"For with God nothing shall be impossible. ~ Luke 1:37

Prayer

Lord, I thank You for Your grace and mercy and for keeping a hedge of protection over me and uplifting my family during our darkest moments. Thank You, Lord, for Your faithfulness and lovingkindness for bringing us through the traumatic experiences, allowing us to testify to Your will and mercy. It is this that gives us the strength to share with Your children. Lord, I ask that You be the source of strength for those who are struggling with suicide or need balance in their life. I ask that You wipe away the spirit of confusion and fear and replace it with courage and strength. Through Jesus' name, I pray. Amen!

Songs of Inspiration

"You Don't Know" ~ Zacadi Cortez
"Gracefully Broken" ~ Tasha Cobbs-Leonard

Family Secrets and Mysteries

Hiding Trauma...

Some people believe burying their trauma will make it go away. Perhaps it relieves them of the pain at the moment.

But when it resurfaces, it brings pain to you and the entire family. Even when it hurts, be honest and transparent. This will help you in ways more than you realize.

It was the early 1980s, and I was approximately seven years old. I was outside playing hopscotch with my neighborhood friends, Tamia and Quana. As the ice cream truck approached our block, Tamia yelled, "Mom! Mom! Can I get ice cream?!" Often I heard my friends say, "Mom." It was times like this when I yearned for my mother and to call her mom.

Other times, I would go into deep thoughts about my mother. I recall Blue Magic's "Land of Make Believe" playing. I went into deep thought, something I had often done. Remembering times my mother dropped my sister and me off at my great-aunt Bertha's house to stay the night while she hung out with her friends. She usually returned to pick us up the next day. Their voices were magical, flawless, and passionate. I was young, so this was not my choice of music. Yet it captured my soul and took me to the make-believe place as I closed my eyes and lived in my fantasy.

I thought of my mother, wishing I could go to the place where she was. I just wanted to be with her and be loved...and feel loved.

I remember inquiring why my mother had never returned to pick up my sister and me. My older cousins were close in age with my mother, so they often shared memories of my mother's genuine love for my sister and me ~ memories of changing our clothing if we got a small stain throughout the day or how she ironed our socks and consoled us. I surmised that something had happened. At the same time, I knew my mother had not abandoned my sister and me; somehow, I needed confirmation.

Aunt Bertha, who had cared for my mother since her teenage years, was now the legal guardian for my sister and me. She had never given me the story of what happened to my mother. Every time I asked, she said she had died, but I did not recall attending a funeral or hearing anyone else speak about my mother's death. It was confusing. My mother had always returned to pick us up, and I could not understand why my mother had not returned this time. I was too young to understand that losing a loved one meant never seeing or talking to that person again. No one ever explained it to me.

It must have been difficult for my Aunt Bertha and my mother's sister Aunt Corey to speak of my mother. I suppose I was too young to know the details, so my aunt felt it best to conceal the story. Perhaps, had my family explained what happened to my mother, I may have had worse experiences. However, my not knowing did not change that I grew up stressed and in despair.

Due to my mother becoming Muslim and joining the Islamic community, my sister and I spoke fluent Arabic. We did not consume pork until my Aunt Bertha and Uncle Clay forced us. Never mind our immune system rejecting their choice of food. After constantly vomiting, we were expected to eat it anyway. While we held onto the little tradition we gained from our mother, eventually, they took that away when we were forced to stop conversing in Arabic.

I cried endless nights, but no one was ever empathetic toward me except my Aunt Veronica and her daughters. It is not that Aunt Bertha did not love us. I presume she did the best she could, especially being diabetic. She was sick most of the time; nonetheless, she did her best to love us by protecting us. For instance, we had to rush into the house if vans drove around the neighborhood. It was strange and scary at that time I did not fully understand why. I do not know if it was due to my Uncle Clay's paranoia that someone was trying to kidnap us. We were not allowed to hang around unfamiliar Muslims either. While the former may not have been peculiar, the latter made me curious. It felt like something more was happening that I was unaware of.

Aunt Bertha and Uncle Clay protected us from the outside world. However, they did feel comfortable allowing us to spend weekends in Hays Homes Projects with my Aunt Veronica and her daughters. These were the exciting times of my childhood. During the summer, my aunt Veronica took us downtown Newark to shop at Woolworth and other stores we did not regularly get to shop from. It was usually hot and crowded, with lots of adults and children passing in every direction. I would scope out all the Muslim women wearing their hijab to see who had my facial features. I wanted to see who would make eye contact with me, wondering if any of them were my mother. It was difficult to tell with those who wore their veil. But if one stared at me long enough, I would think she wanted to reveal herself and say, "Hey baby, Mommy misses you so much."

That never happened.

Stress and Despair

Where was God in all of this?

Why was what happened to my mother such a mystery? I received insight into my family's history later in life. I began pulling the pieces together.

Scripture

"I waited patiently for the Lord; he turned to me and heard my cry... He set my feet on a rock and gave me a firm place to stand." ~ Psalm 40:1-2

"Lord, you know the hopes of the helpless. Surely you will hear their cries and comfort them." ~ Psalm 10:17

Prayer

Lord, I thank You for the time I spent with my mother; although it was brief, I am grateful for the memories others shared. Thank You for hearing my cry and comforting me during the good and challenging times. Lord, I thank You for every experience, easy and difficult, and for allowing me to rely on You to bring me out of those difficult circumstances and showing me the glory on the other side. God, I thank You for standing firmly with me even when I did not know to call on You. Great is your mercy. Thank You for surrounding me with each and every relative who was able to detail positive experiences of my mother that I was able to create memories through them. Through Jesus Christ, I pray. Amen!

Songs of Inspiration

"Great Is Your Mercy" ~ Donnie McClurkin

"We Gon' Be Alright" ~ Tye Tribbett

"In the Midst Of It All" ~ Yolanda Adams

Mother's Murder

My significant loss…

The person who birthed me, who was always supposed to be there for me, and who loved me unconditionally is now gone.

Following the separation of my mother and father, my mother eventually converted to Islam. Eventually, she became involved with Sal. He was a Muslim man who allegedly manipulated and mentally abused my mother. Although I am unsure of every detail, relatives informed me that when I was a toddler, my mother traveled to her hometown in Georgia to visit her siblings.

According to Aunt Corey, my mother left my sister and me in New Jersey during that visit. Before her return to New Jersey, my mother promised Aunt Corey that she would return within a few months to support Aunt Corey with her children.

Little did Aunt Corey know that would mark the last embrace, laughter, touch, and conversation she would have with her sister (my mother). As a child and throughout my adulthood, relatives have speculated about what happened to my mother; each story corroborated the other.

Allegedly, Sal killed some woman and dismembered the body. Supposedly during the time my mother was missing, there were reports of a man leaving the Colonnade Projects in Newark with blood dripping from his suitcase. It was alleged that the man fled to New York with the luggage, and police captured him crossing the George Washington Bridge. The police found the dismembered body of a female in his luggage.

Although hurtful to know, my family hoped this would bring closure to their dreadful hearts, but the remains were found to be that of another woman Sal was involved with, not my mother. Unfortunately, my mother's body was never found, or at least that is what I was told through the years. As frightening as that may sound, with my mother's disappearance, my sister and I remained with the alleged murderer. I do not know the length of time or if there were other caretakers, as it was alleged that Sal was involved with multiple women. Nevertheless, Sal physically abused my sister and me, none of which I remember. These reports came from relatives who revealed that our heads were bruised as if he hit us on the crown of our heads as punishment. I learned from an older cousin that we had sores on our heads and feet from Sal beating us, perhaps as a disciplinary measure.

The abuse may have carried on until the day he called my family to pick us up. Well, not exactly that kind of a gesture. It sort of went like this... "You better come to get them, or they will be next." After my Aunt Bertha and Uncle Clay pleaded with him not to hurt us, he directed my Uncle Clay and Aunt Bertha to meet him to retrieve us. It was alleged that when my Aunt Bertha and Uncle Clay arrived, we stood alone on the dark street, but there were headlights from a car in the distance. He made a quick getaway.

The trauma we endured living with my mother's boyfriend, Sal, impacted our stay with my Aunt Bertha. The harsh discipline imposed by Sal resulted in us hiding in the closet at Aunt Bertha's house whenever we thought we were in trouble.

I recall another version of my older cousin telling me that Aunt Bertha and Uncle Clay visited my sister and me at our apartment in the projects. At that time, my mother had been missing for some days. So my mother's sister asked Aunt Bertha to pick us up from my mother's boyfriend then, and that was the breadth of the discussion.

Gotta Move On

Despite all this trauma, we had to move forward as usual. We went to school and were expected to behave as if nothing was wrong.

Scripture

"What the devil meant for harm, God
meant for Good." ~ Genesis 50:20

"For I know the thoughts that I think toward for
you, saith the Lord, thoughts of peace and not of evil
to give you an expected end." ~ Jeremiah 29:11

"Thanks be to God, who delivers me through
Jesus Christ our Lord!" ~ Romans 7:25

Prayer

Lord, I thank You for the hedge of protection You kept over me throughout my life. Although there were some painful years, days, and nights, it could have been worse. You said what the devil meant for harm You meant for good. God, allow your people to see your glory just as You have allowed me. Lord, thank You for allowing me to step into Your plans that You have for me to prosper. Thank You for Your presence in my past, present, and future. I am grateful and do not want to take any of it for granted. Lord, I ask that You keep me humble as You continue to take me along the journey You have for me. Thank You for giving me Your expected end. Through Christ. Amen!

Song of Inspiration:

"He Has His Hands On You" ~ Marvin Sapp

Dr. Fatima A. McCoy-Leonard

The Sister's Great Escape

About 20 years later...

When times get hard, some people get to running. Perhaps some people just like to escape their reality and look for opportunities to start anew. Maybe that was what Aunt Mae's goal was. Who knew she would abandon her family?

Endurance through hard times is a test of your loyalty, strength, and faith.

During my adult years, I learned that my family's history of trauma began long before my sister's suicide attempt or my mother's disappearance. Eventually, I learned that when my mother was a child, she had lost her mother to a horrific car accident. So motherless and fatherless, my great-grandfather took legal guardianship of all seven of his grandchildren, my mother, and her young siblings.

My mother was a young girl at the time. In fact, all of her siblings were underage except her one sister Aunt Mae, a young adult about 13 years older than my mother. She was old enough to care for the family. Instead, she decided to move to a different coast and start anew. Little did her siblings know that starting anew would mean they would never see nor hear from Aunt Mae again. When my great-grandfather fell ill, my mother, as a teenager, sought the opportunity to grow in a different environment. Then, she migrated to New Jersey with her mother's sister (my great-aunt, Bertha).

I was told that shortly following my grandmother's death, my mother's eldest sister, Aunt Mae, spontaneously moved from Georgia to California with two of her small children. She allegedly sought the opportunity to create a better life for herself. Especially since she bore four children in her early adulthood. The family did not know that would be the last they would see or hear from her.

I had never met Aunt Mae; however, my Aunt Corey told me of her existence when I visited in adolescence. Although my Aunt Corey did not give details about her sister (my Aunt Mae, who moved to California), I always wanted to go to California to meet her and my cousins. I fantasized about going to California and lying on the beach, playing in the sand and water with my family, but that never became a reality. Eventually, I stopped inquiring about when we would visit Aunt Mae in California. Now again, just as I used to fantasize about being with my mother, I fantasized about being amongst my Aunt Mae and cousins.

Years later, I had a jaw-dropping moment when I received a phone call from an unexpected person I never knew existed. Around 2019, a woman named Gloria called my phone, claiming to be my cousin. I had never met her or, for that matter, even heard of her before the phone call. Nevertheless, she captured my attention by mentioning the names of relatives I am familiar with. It was through that conversation that I learned she was my first cousin. It was one of the daughters of my Aunt Mae. Well, this was a revelation to me. I remembered hearing that Aunt Mae lived in California with her children. Unbeknownst to me, my Aunt Mae had two other children she had left behind fifty years prior.

All Glory Be to God

Stop running away from your trauma and work through it. Sometimes I wondered why I had so many hardships; God always answered, *I am strengthening you.*

Things may have turned out differently had my Aunt Mae never left. I will probably not have these life experiences to share with you. God is intentional and will not put more on you than you can bear.

Scripture

"Acquaint now thyself with him and be at peace:
thereby good shall come unto thee." ~ Job 22:21-22

"Thou shalt make thy prayer unto him, and he shall
hear thee, and thy shall pay thou vows." ~ Job 27:30
"Great is the Lord, and greatly to be praised, and
his greatness is unsearchable." ~ Psalm 145:3

Prayer

Lord, I thank You for giving me the strength to endure
difficult times. It is easy to run away, to try to escape the
trauma and tumultuous times, but God, I ask that you give
me faith the size of a mustard seed and make me faithful
like Job. Give Your children the wisdom to know that faith is
the substance of things hoped for, the evidence of things not
seen. Therefore knowing when times get hard, You can turn
it around. God, You said the burden is not ours but the Lord's.
Allow Your children to let go and allow You to do Your work
in them. God, thank You for keeping Your hands on me. I give
You all the glory and grace. Through Christ, I pray. Amen!

Song of Inspiration

"You Deserve It" ~ JJ Hairston & Youthful Praise

Denial

Random Phone Call Revelations...

So remember, in the previous chapter, I learned my grandmother died in a car accident. Many years later, I discovered that was part of the truth.

Although my cousin Gloria is my first cousin, she and my mother were a few years apart and had grown up together. She would be the person to bridge the gap between secrets and truth.

After meeting my older cousin, Gloria, I was told that the McCoy family in Georgia was one of the poorest families in town. Hearing this made it even more important for me to hold onto my last name. I am proud of my name and the legacy God is allowing me to create to change the trajectory of how people will remember the McCoy bloodline from about a century ago.

A lot of hidden secrets came out by meeting cousin Gloria. I already knew that my grandmother (mother's mother) had eight children and was raising them as a single mother. I later learned she had returned from a long workday and went to the store. On her route home from the store, a man she had known offered her a ride home. It was said that after she entered his vehicle, the man tried to rape or raped her. She escaped the vehicle which led the man to run her over, dismembering her body. Her helpless body lay on the road until paramedics arrived.

As years passed, I discovered that my Aunt Mae, who moved to California and left with two of her younger children, disowned her siblings and her other two daughters, including my cousin

Gloria. Unbelievable!!! Needless to say, none of my family attended counseling to resolve the past trauma.

For years my cousin Gloria searched for her mother (Aunt Mae). After many attempts to make contact, during the summer of 2021, my cousin, sister, and I finally spoke with my Aunt Mae's youngest daughter, who was born in California. She had no knowledge of us or the truth about her family from Georgia that her mother had left behind 50 years prior. Without shame, while on the phone with her, my Aunt Mae denied having other children back home and even denied her daughter Gloria to her face and discontinued communication. After leaving her hometown, my Aunt Mae never called or returned home to visit. She had even kept her two children she left behind a secret. We spoke with Aunt Mae, but she denied knowing Gloria. We thought that finding Aunt Mae would bring relief to our broken family; instead, it created more heartache.

Out of all the family hardships and trauma, somehow, I realized that God was with me and guiding me along the way.

Betrayal

When the pain of abandonment, denial, and betrayal kick in, remember Mark 14:72, when Jesus spoke with His disciples.

Jesus Christ, who was a perfect person, endured the ultimate betrayal. So who are we that we will not endure heartbreak and rejection? Jesus' disciples, who witnessed Jesus make miracles happen, denied Him and watched Jesus be crucified.

If it can happen to the perfect man, no one is exempt from experiencing heartache and strife. It is a matter of how you choose to receive it and move forward from it. Jesus' testimony proves that we will endure pain and betrayal, but God promised joy in the mourning!

Scripture

"Truly, I tell you. This very night, before the rooster crows twice, you will deny me three times." ~ Mark 14:72

"He healeth the broken in heart and bindeth up their wounds." ~ Psalm 147:3

Prayer

God, You did not say that life would be easy. Although people may deny me, I thank You for always claiming me as Your child. People have denied Jesus Christ even after they witnessed His miracles. So I expect people to turn against me. But Lord, I thank You for keeping me in perfect peace. Lord, I ask that You heal the hearts and souls of those who are broken. Mend their hearts, Lord, so that they can move past their trauma. I ask these prayers through Christ. Amen!

Songs of Inspiration

"Gracefully Broken" ~ Tasha Cobbs-Leonard

"I Almost Let Go" ~ Kurt Carr

Abandonment

~∘⬭✺⬮∘~

Daddy, where are you?...

As if at four years old, dealing with the loss of my mother was not enough; I had to cope with abandonment from my father.

I could always feel the pain my father was experiencing with the loss of my mother and his children. It must have been too painful for him to endure and show up for us.

Although a military veteran, when I was a toddler, my father lived a life of crime, leading to his incarceration. Consequently, when the turmoil surrounding my mother's disappearance came to light, he was unaware.

As a child, I did not have the self-awareness to relate my unhappiness to my trauma. I just was not a happy child. Some years ago, during my adulthood, I recall my cousin telling me I used to be a mean kid and never smiled. To prove this point, we looked at photographs from my childhood, and he was correct. I was not smiling in any of the photographs.

Although I was with my father infrequently, the happiest times during my childhood were when I was with my father. As a child, I always revered my father as my hero. He was tall, slender, fearless, and intelligent. He would pick me up and make me feel like I could touch the sky.

When I was about six or seven years old, there were periods when my father consistently picked my sister and me up for the weekend. Although we were always excited to be with my father, his addiction to alcohol and drugs prevented him from showing up as frequently as he should have. I experienced numerous broken promises as I always looked forward to my father keeping his word...he did not.

Nevertheless, one of the greatest joys was gaining a stepmother. I developed a relationship with my stepmother Wanda and her daughter. My stepmother was the womanly figure I needed. She showed me unconditional love and always gave me affection and care. Although my grandmother Hattie (father's mother) was the first woman aside from my mother to say, "I love you," Mommy Wanda made me feel loved. Not that I did not feel loved by my grandmother. It was different hearing it and receiving physical affection from Mommy Wanda. She even kissed me on my lips, how I frequently observed mothers engage with their daughters. She was my mother in the absence of my biological mother.

I would get my hopes up of spending more time with my father and Mommy Wanda, but my father could not push himself to come around for months. It was very inconsistent, but the love was never lost.

After enduring what is known as complex trauma, my sister and I had not received counseling as children. Not to mention, the public school system during the 1980s surely did not lead with social-emotional support. Instead, there was a system of corporal punishment. I was punished when I displayed anger or withdrawal from my learning. I remember my second-grade teacher telling the class to call me 'Evel Knievel.' I did not know who that person was, but I knew it was out of disdain for how I behaved during that time. So it could not have been a good thing.

Although I grew up in a large family, I felt there was no place for me. The three-bedroom apartment was overcrowded with eleven of my cousins, my Uncle Clay, and Aunt Bertha. Other than my sister, there was no one with whom I shared the same last name. So I carried the pain when my older cousin would playfully say, "We found y'all in the garbage can." Or when my uncle would say, "Your father ain't sh*#."

No matter the length of time my father was away, I found great joy when he came around. I had a sense of belonging and protection I deeply needed, especially from the predator who lived amongst me. There had been rumors whispered in the apartment that Uncle Clay had fathered his stepdaughter's child. I am unsure if that is true; however, when Cousin Effie had mental breakdowns, she cussed everyone out and tore her room apart. She would have piles of clothes thrown about her room and huge red cars drawn on her bedroom walls. I would hear whispering gossip about her having one of her mental moments. I was too young to understand what was going on. I just knew it was frightening to see and hear. Apparently, the whispering was about how Uncle Clay messed her head up doing whatever he did to her.

Whatever that was, I guess I was his next prey.

I must have been about ten years old when Uncle Clay hit me on my right arm with a wire hanger that punctured my skin. Blood dripped from my arm while he told me to shut up from crying. The most I could say was, "I hate you!" I still wear the scar on my arm. Sometimes you will live with the physical scars as well as the mental and emotional scars.

Aside from the physical abuse, there were times Uncle Clay would wake me up for school by wrapping his arms and hands around my small bulging breast that were developing and pulling me out of bed. This made me feel uncomfortable and disgusted, but there was nothing I could do except tell him to get off me.

Another occasion of Uncle Clay's predatory behavior was when I was about twelve, and diabetes landed my Aunt Bertha in the hospital. Her absence from the household left my uncle in charge. This was when he propositioned me with $40 to suck my breast. Although I declined the offer, I was so embarrassed to tell anyone at the time. I gained the courage to say something the night we found out my Aunt Bertha had died. I angrily blurted it out. Of course, my uncle denied the claim saying, "I would not pay my dog to suck your breast." My cousin laughed hysterically; I guess it was just that funny. To me, it was painful and embarrassing, yet liberating. Noone confronted my uncle Clay about my accusation.

I knew I needed my father's protection for times like this. The one person who was so strong and powerful but was suffering silently in his addiction and was not mentally present during that time of my life. Aunt Bertha never made it home from the hospital. She died in the hospital a few days after being admitted.

Here I was, a child expected to move on with life as usual without emotional support in or outside the household. I suppose all the suppressed trauma impacted my sister's mental health during our adolescent years resulting in her suicide attempt.

Forgiveness

The storm does not always last. My pastor said once is not always, and always is not forever. I always had a forgiving heart for my father. My discernment allowed me to feel and understand his love for my sister and me. He always told us, and we felt it in his presence.

Scripture

"For if ye forgive men their trespasses, your heavenly Father will also forgive you." ~ Matthew 6:14

"Forbearing one another, and forgiving one another, even as Christ forgave you." ~ Colossians 3:13

Prayer

Lord, I did not always know that better days were coming. Thank You for giving me the spirit of forgiveness. Lord, just as You said that You would forgive us, thank You for allowing me to forgive those who have hurt or wronged me in any way. Holding on to the hurt and grudges only prevents me from making space for the blessing You have for me. God, although I had to deal with loss and abandonment, I know You brought me through. Thank you, Lord! Amen.

Songs of Inspiration

"Better Days" ~ Le'Andia Johnson

"Never Would Have Made It" ~ Marvin Sapp

Remember, forgiveness is for you!

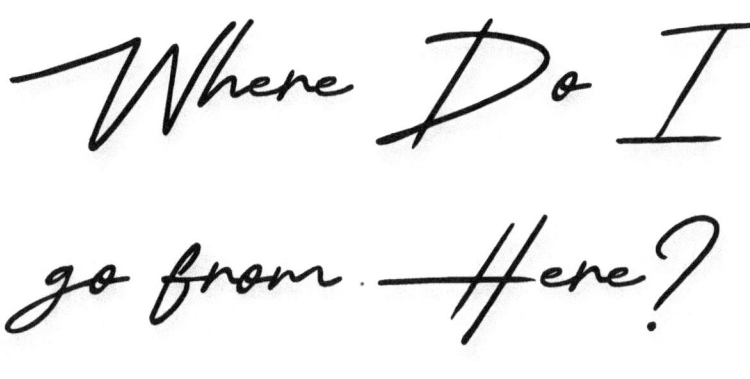

Where Do I go from Here?

Survival Mode...

Although I subconsciously forgave my father, he continued to be absent. Now his mother stepped up to take over guardianship.

My grandmother Hattie was not an affectionate caregiver, but I knew she loved me. She was a provider and worked arduously to ensure her family was cared for. I must have been about 12 years old when my aunt Bertha died, and I wondered who would take responsibility for my sister and me.

With no one else around us to pick up the pieces, we called our grandmother Hattie. Without hesitation, she took custody which meant that I had to relocate during my pivotal adolescent years. Maybe it was a blessing that I got out of the environment I was in.

This was the time of my life when I practically had to fend for myself. My grandmother took custody, but she lived out of town, miles away. So my sister and I were left in the care of our uncles during our junior high school years. I loved my uncles, but I could not relate to them.

Eventually, my Uncle Greg died from AIDS, which was extremely traumatic to witness; however, I am happy I had the opportunity to spend time with him. He was the artistic fun uncle but succumbed to the street life, which made his time short with us.

While I viewed my Uncle Mike as the serious nerdy uncle, he stayed in the house with us, so there was always an adult present until he was fatally killed in a robbery turned murder. I remember Uncle Mike leaving for work; he told my sister and me to order food so that we would have dinner for the night, and he would reimburse us when he returned home. The day never came. Days later, it was reported that he was found dead in the street.

With a lack of consistent supervision, I began to experiment with marijuana. I would sit and smoke with my friends at the time. One day we had an epiphany, why don't we sell weed to make money? Collectively, we decided that we could not get high off our own supply, so we stopped smoking and began selling. Now we had money.

We teamed up and became partners. I took my first entrepreneurial experience seriously. We had a Jamaican connect who we purchased pounds of weed from. We bagged up and sold it after school and on the weekends. Our business flourished quickly (at least it seemed; in hindsight, it was petty cash), so we had to leave some of the goods with an older friend to sell while we were in school.

Now we had to worry about "stick up kids" (people committing armed robbery). No worries for us. The local drug dudes kept us protected.

This lasted about six months. I do not know how we concluded to end our illegal business. We definitely did not think about the dangers of doing so, but thank God we came out unscathed. It had to be God. Then, I began surrounding myself with a new set of friends considered "good girls." We would just run around like kids and ring doorbells and run.

Repent Your Sins

It is never too late to ask God for forgiveness of your sins. This was my sin which is no more of a sin than any other sin you may have committed.

Do not judge me for my indiscretions. God said, "Judge not." Your sin is no less of a sin than mine. Instead, ask yourself, "Have I asked God for forgiveness of my sins?"

Scripture

"Although I want to do good, evil is right
there with me." ~ Romans 7:21

"Judge not, that ye be not judged. For with what judgment
ye judge, ye shall be judged: and with what measure ye
mete, it shall be measured to you again." ~ Matthew 7:1

"The spirit is willing, but the flesh is weak." ~ Matthew 26:41

Prayer

God, thank You for giving me direction when I went
down the wrong path. Thank You for not allowing me to
stay there. You told us our flesh is weak, so thank You
for allowing me to be more like You. Lord, thank You
for allowing me to walk by faith, not sight. Thank You
for allowing me to appreciate the things I have and to
understand that material things are meaningless. Thank
You for allowing me to walk in the spirit of Christ. Amen.

Songs of Inspiration

"Change Me" ~ Tamela Mann
"Grateful" ~ Hezekiah Walker

Let Downs and Disappointments

<hr />

Strengthening Me...

What will you sacrifice?

I have had many letdowns and disappointments throughout my life. Not just from my father's abandonment but severed friendships and hardships in my career. I had to trust that God would keep me in perfect peace and that something greater was on the horizon for me.

My testimony to you is there will be many people who will let you down. The letdowns may come unexpectedly from the people you admire and expect to show up for you the most.

Just trust God and His process.

Although painful not having my father present during my crucial childhood and adolescence, I forgave him and continued to move forward with my life. Similarly, in my adulthood, I moved forward when people seemingly acted as if they had my best interest but showed they did not really care about me or my success. This was painful, especially when this behavior came from those I admired. Therefore, I tell you regardless of whether someone shows up for you, you have to continue moving forward in the direction God is leading you to accomplish your goal.

God has supplied you with everything you need. You have all the strength and courage needed to do the things you set forth to do. That is already in your favor; you must step out and get it. Do not worry about how it looks. In the end, you will see the results that you are looking for.

You may even have friends who will let you down. Sometimes the people who you roll with the most become your adversary. They may even start competing with you. Just know the only person you should compete with is yourself. Always strive to be a better person. Remember, there is no competition in friendship. Friends always seek to build one another up. If you look good, you should certainly want your friends to look just as good. Help elevate one another. When that is not reciprocated, it may be time to separate yourself from the person not adding value to your life. God will begin to lead you in another direction, limiting or forcing you to cease interactions with that person. I had to sever ties in friendships. It was not easy until I realized that God was controlling the outcome.

God separates us from people for a reason. We have to learn to accept where God is taking us. Sometimes instead of paying attention to the signs God is showing us, we may resist not being friends or not being invited out. Sometimes God will bring you back together. Sometimes, you may never recapture what once was. You must be okay with that.

What are you willing to sacrifice? When God calls you, what are you ready to give up to answer His call? Are you willing to separate yourself from the people you surround yourself with to do what God would have you do? Are you willing to give up friendships or relationships that keep you distracted from God?

Tapping Into My Purpose

Scripture

"To everything there is a season and a time to every purpose under the heaven." ~ Ecclesiastes: 3:1

Prayer

Lord, You are an intentional God. Thank You for giving me the insight I need to know when to move out of Your way and allow You to do Your work. Lord, thank You for the change in friendships, knowing that everything has a season and purpose. Even when I wanted to hold on to people, You strategically removed them from my life to prepare me for the journey You designed for me. Thank You for giving me the wherewithal to know that separating me from people, places, and circumstances is part of Your plan to use me to do Your work. Lord, thank You for allowing me to be alright when You separate me from people who are a distraction for me. Thank You for keeping me focused on doing Your work, O Lord. Through Christ. Amen!

Song of Inspiration

"He's Intentional" ~ Travis Greene

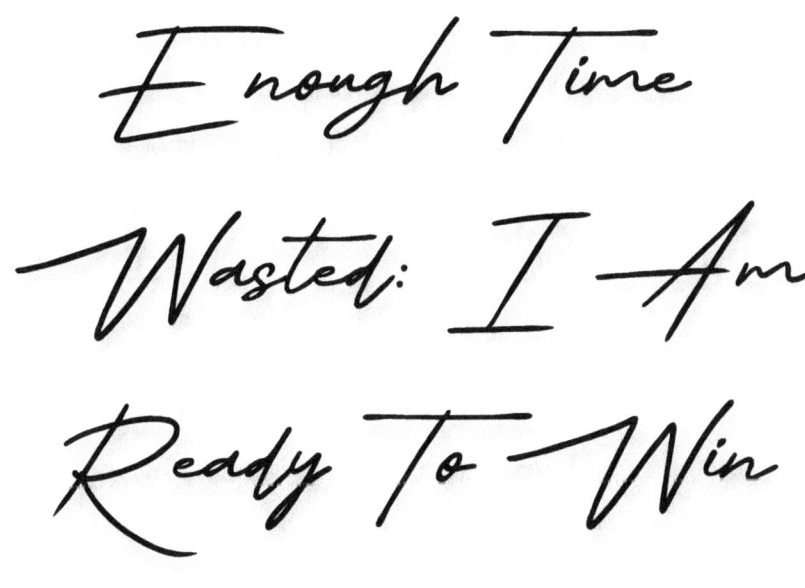

Enough Time Wasted: I Am Ready To Win

Overcoming the invisible obstacle of Imposter Syndrome and stepping into greatness!

Getting out of the way, not letting fear win.

How do I get out of my way? This is the most challenging question I have ever asked myself.

You tend to engage in self-doubt or personal incompetence when you have been told you are nothing and never will be anything.

During my childhood, I lacked a voice and self-confidence. Subconsciously negative thoughts from my childhood impacted my adolescent years and adulthood—thoughts of that little girl whose self-confidence was diminished every time she was told she was stupid or to shut up. It decided to visit me in adulthood. It showed up as Imposter Syndrome.

According to Simply Psychology, Imposter Syndrome refers to an internal experience of self-doubt and believing you are not as competent as others perceive you to be. Despite the objective success in education, experiences, or accomplishments, it is characterized by chronic feelings of fraudulent incompetence and inadequacy (Frothingham, 24, April 2023). Although I reached the pinnacle of education, I sometimes questioned my ability to accomplish goals. I decided that the Imposter Syndrome stalled me for far too long. I had become accustomed to dreaming big and feeling like I could not obtain those goals. I would remain a dreamer until I finally decided that I was equipped to fulfill my desires. Although I was never a quitter, there were goals I wanted to accomplish that I was afraid to approach. I did not think I had the ability to accomplish them.

Sometimes, I did not think I was smart enough to be in the room with highly intellectual professionals. The only difference between me and them is that they believed in themselves and accomplished bigger dreams than I thought I could. This all stemmed from my childhood. It is amazing how much trauma we carry throughout our lives and do not even realize it.

Are you taking charge of your life?

If you know that Nike slogan "Just Do It," it is time that you start living by that.

Take more action and put less thought into what you want to do. I am not saying that you should act impulsively. You need to think about the goals that you want to accomplish. Nevertheless, if all you do is think about what you want and do not act on it, you will never know your strength. You must act on your thoughts and stop making excuses or reasons why you cannot. It is time for you to get up and do the work God has called you to do, even when you feel stuck or do not know where or how to start.

I am a success story as I came from a poor family and grew up without my parents. Nonetheless, I have earned college degrees, have multiple careers, have a wonderful husband, launched my non-profit organization, purchased real estate, and embraced my spirituality. People look at my accomplishments and commend me for being a positive force. Yet, there is a yearning in me to do more.

Through reflection, I know I am not living my fullest potential. Sometimes I feel frustrated with myself for not pushing myself to do more in the time that I have lived thus far. No matter how much greatness people saw in me, there were times that I sat with imposter syndrome. I would feel like I was not good enough or deserving of all the greatness God blessed me with. This is consequently due to how I was raised. I was always hushed and not allowed to speak my thoughts freely without being judged or told to be quiet. As a child, I always felt that I did not matter.

Do you always need affirmation? Take a moment and think about that.

Why do I hold onto fear like it will propel me forward? There were times that I felt stuck, not literally, subconsciously. I did not know how to break free. Then God told me, "If you never had to struggle, you would not have the story to tell." I give my testimonies to encourage others who are in the fight and cannot see the light. Because I made it through, you should know that it is possible.

Imposter No More

Scripture

"I can do all things through Christ which
strengthens me." ~ Philippians 4:13

"Fear thou not, for I am with thee: be not dismayed; for
I am thy God: I will strengthen thee." ~ Isaiah 41:10

"For I the thoughts I think toward you. Saith
the Lord, thoughts of peace and not of evil to
give you an expected end." ~Jeremiah 29:11

"The LORD is my shepherd; I shall not want." ~ Psalm 23:1

Songs of Inspiration

"Be Blessed" ~ Yolanda Adams

"When I Pray" ~ Doe

"Hello Fear" ~ Kirk Franklin

"Break Every Chain" ~ Tamela Mann

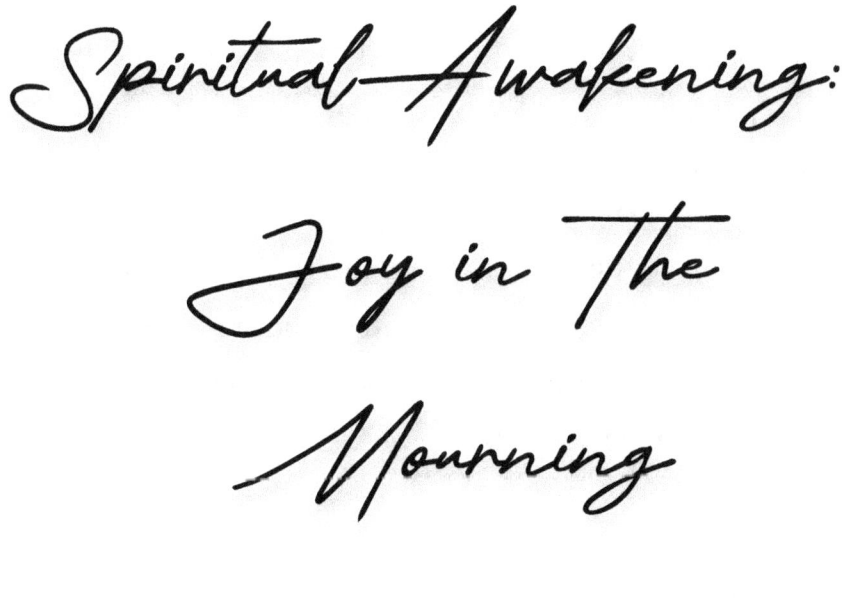

Spiritual Awakening: Joy in The Mourning

Letting go...

When I tell you, I do not look like what I have been through. I have not allowed the trauma and pain to consume my life moving forward. In 2016 I gave my life to Christ and put my faith in the Lord. I trust that God will do what He said he would.

Let go of negative thoughts. Let go of shame, toxicity, guilt, cruelty, doubt, fear, and grudges, even in toxic relationships.

These things are holding you hostage.

Through all the stress and turmoil I have experienced, God was leading me through it to something greater than I had ever anticipated.

I kept having the desire to attend church and to do community service. I just could not decide on which church to attend. I visited a couple of churches. During that time, my cousin invited me to her church for Sunday service. After visiting a couple of times, I decided to join.

Often I dreamt about events in my life that had manifested. The desires kept pouring in. I wanted to commit my life to service, and God strategically removed people from my life who were distractions and gave me clear focus. God then aligned me with people who supported my journey.

I had a friend I thought we would be friends forever; God kept warning me to let go, yet I ignored the signs. They were subtle signs that were waved off as nothing much. I felt like God kept giving me the signs, which I ignored until one day, God made it blatantly obvious that we had served the purpose in each other's lives. This is not to say that I am better than or she is better than. We were no longer aligned and walking in different directions, so God separated us. This may be to prevent deterrence or distraction by the people around you when you need to stay on course.

God said there is a season for everything. God will place people in your life during a particular time, maybe to get through something; whatever the situation is, everyone is not meant to go on your journey with you. God will remove the people from around you who are not supposed to be with you. It was a hard lesson for me. No matter how much you think you know someone, everyone does not mean you well. Sometimes jealousy and enmity show up in relationships, and we must discern when to move on and away from those individuals.

In 2016 I got baptized and gave my life to Christ. There is victory at the end of the dark tunnel. My story continues...

Joy In The Mourning

Do not be consumed by painful experiences. Learn the needed lesson and move forward in glorifying God, for He is strengthening you.

Scripture

"And blessed is he, whosoever shall not be offended in me." ~ Matthew 11:6

"For my yoke is easy, and my burden is light." ~ Matthew 11:30

"God can do exceedingly and abundantly above all beyond what you can ask for." ~ Ephesians 3:20-21

Songs of Inspiration

"Let Go, Let God" ~ PJ Morton featuring The Walls Group

"He Turned It" ~ Tye Tribett

Renewed Faith

God is calling you. Pay attention to the signs. Sometimes the signs come in the form of dreams or through unexpected people. To get your attention, God may send messages through people you may not expect to deliver the message. Or there are times God may show up through your dreams.

I was a little girl when God showed up in my dream. I remember being in the sky, and God put wings on me. I only told one person about that dream about five years ago. In January of 2023, I had a similar dream where God put the wings on me with a rocketship attached. This was God telling me He was with me then and carried me through my journey. Even during those times, I allowed imposter syndrome to slow me down. Nevertheless, God never left me. Now, God is propelling me forward at a high velocity to get me caught up to where He needs me to be.

Although I knew God was with me, I continued to experience spiritual warfare. I was attacked in my friendships, my relationship, and my career. Sometimes it may be difficult to discern if God is speaking to you, even more so what the message is that God wants you to receive. Prayer provides me with clarity and direction.

Naturally, through my reflection on my past, I asked God for forgiveness. I requested forgiveness for all the times I procrastinated on moving forward with a goal. More or less, fear prevented me. I wanted to control the process. I wanted to be involved in every step of the way and how it looked. From that moment, I knew I needed to move out of my own way.

Have you ever heard someone say, let go and let God? Sure, we say it, but how many of us truly do it?

I would say it but never relinquished. It is the same in relationships or any experiences you have. If you continue to do the same things in the same way, the result will always be the same. Yet, somehow, we look forward to different results. So when I moved out of the way, I took the guidance and made significant progress.

You may ask yourself, *how will I know the path God is directing me*? You will know in your heart and spirit. As God prepares you for your transition or elevation, you may begin feeling uncomfortable where you are or that the odds are against you. Or you may begin to do things without much thought about what to do. Sometimes, I received messages in my dreams.

That's how I knew. Other times, I received messages from unexpected people. People I did not speak with frequently or who knew nothing of me personally would mention things they would not otherwise have known other than God speaking through them.

Scripture

"Ask, and it shall be given you; seek and ye shall find; knock, and it shall be opened unto you." ~ Matthew 7:7

"And all things, whatsoever ye shall ask in prayer, believing, ye shall receive." ~ Matthew 21:22

"So then faith comes by hearing, and hearing by the word of God." ~ Romans 10:17

Songs of Inspiration

"God's Got A Blessing" ~ Norman Hutchins

"Wanna Be Happy" ~ Kirk Franklin

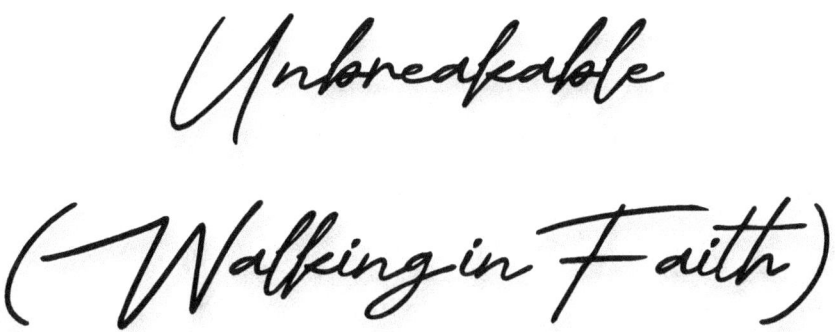

Unbreakable

(Walking in Faith)

They denied you your raise; God never left you fruitless.

They denied you for the promotion; God's timing is perfect.

They said you are not good enough; God said you are perfect.

They gossiped about you and spread false rumors; let your haters motivate you.

And remember, lions don't care about the comments of sheep.

Winning even when the enemy did not know I would...

God definitely took me through the struggle. Nothing has ever come easy for me. My pastor recited a quote by Aristotle, "Patience is bitter, but its fruit is sweet." Your journey may have been difficult, stressful, and long but the rewards for enduring are insurmountable.

Sometimes we go through something to grow. Like a pearl, we come out on the other side with grace and mercy. The oyster covers up when an intruder enters inside it. God covers us when things occur in our lives that bring us pain. Oh, but when we come out on the other side, we should glorify His name.

Spiritual Warfare...

I have unwavering faith in God. As God pushes me in one direction, the devil always attacks me and tries to take me off course. I say this so that you understand you may be in spiritual warfare. Stay in prayer. The devil only comes to steal, kill, and destroy, literally and figuratively. Do not allow the devil to steal your joy or dreams.

When you feel doubt and are ready to give up, remember your "why." Ask yourself, "Why am I doing this?" This will give you the reset you may need to stay on course. Some people see my success yet have no idea it was obtainable, but not without effort and time. Keep knocking on the door if it is for you. It will eventually open. I did not always pass the qualifying exam on

DR. FATIMA A. MCCOY-LEONARD

the first attempt. Nor did I always get the promotion I wanted on the first interview. Eventually, I got it because it was for me.

Sometimes God was not ready to open the door. Just know that no one can close a door that God has opened, and no one has the ability to open a door God has closed. So stop giving people that much power in your life. Therefore, praying and asking God to align your desires with what he wants for you is important.

This is not an attempt to boast or showcase my accomplishments. This is so that you can see the greatness of God when you remain faithful. I guess you can say that I am the personification of resilience. Despite obstacles, I have always been determined to overcome barriers and accomplish my goals. So I will say that I have not failed anything. Instead, I have lived experiences that have strengthened me.

You, too, can see things in this light. Remember, if God be for you, who can be against you? Let go of that bitterness, strife, and anger toward other people. You are harboring it and allowing it to weigh you down. God is moving you into a season of greatness where that is not allowed. You must begin to act like it, walk like it, and talk like it. There has to be a paradigm shift in how you approach situations.

God's Timing

Scripture

"To everything, there is a season and a time to every purpose under the heaven." ~ Ecclesiastes 3:1

"Let your light shine before men, that they may see your good works, and glorify your Father which is in heaven." ~ Matthew 5:16

"If God be for us, who can be against us?"~ Romans: 8:31

"No weapon formed against me shall prosper, and every tongue that shall rise against thee in judgment thou shalt condemn." ~ Isaiah 54:17

Songs of Inspiration

"Never Gave Up" ~ JJ Hairston, Travis Greene

"Something Has to Break" ~ Tasha Cobbs-Leonard

"Gracefully Broken" ~ Tasha Cobbs-Leonard

Epilogue

I determined my purpose...

My past did not define my future, but I became determined to pursue my purpose. I had to reflect deeply on what kept me from living abundantly in my purpose. Through my reflection, I learned that as a result of my childhood trauma, I had allowed fear to hold me back. Gratefully, my relationship with God let me know that all I have gone through was preparing me for my purpose.

I have made mistakes in my life and will make many more. However, God is a forgiving God, and in serving God, I have everything my heart desires. Even if it is not yet, I know it is coming. Through my faith in the Lord, I know no one has the power to prevent me from reaping the blessings God has for me.

Although imposter syndrome has come up in the past, it is no longer allowed in my presence.

I have always lived in determination to break down the barriers I faced, which resulted in my success. When one door closed, I knocked on the other. Keep knocking. If it is for you, it will be. Be okay with changes in friendships. When people no longer want to be around you, God is making room for you to be in the good company of others.

Constant gratitude and prayer are the forces that drive me. I did not get to know my mother. She was taken away from me early, so I vaguely remember the time with her. My father was around sporadically. I never got to experience the full love of my parents. I could not control those circumstances but decided to take charge of my life. Thus, I decided not to let my childhood trauma affect my progression. It may not be easy, but you must let go to move forward.

Although my Uncle Clay was mean, and I still wear the scar on my arm from my abuse, I never held a grudge against him. I visited him in the hospital before he died when I was in high school. Holding grudges is like holding yourself hostage to your past. Let Go and Let God fight your battles.

God uses us in ways that we cannot even imagine. We ask God to reveal things to us when we are sometimes not receptive to receiving what He will offer us. Or should I say, sometimes we are not open to how God delivers what we ask of Him?

Once I truly committed my life to God, I discovered that God had revealed Himself in many ways that I had never noticed before. So when we ask, we must be prepared for how God will respond. It will not always be what we want or how we want God to respond, but He is magnificent and will show up.

I always knew that God had directed my life and continued to pour many blessings into my family and me, but I somehow felt a void. There was something that I was seeking but couldn't quite figure out. I wanted to join a church for about three years but always became distracted by worldly things.

Eventually, I reached a point where God began strategically removing people from my life. People whom I have always thought would be in my life forever. Unbeknownst to me, God was preparing me for a journey that I have always wanted but never utilized the potential I had in me to move forward with. I had to understand that God surrounded me with people who would strengthen me and force me to live a life of abundance, and I would be that for them as well.

When that time passed, it was time to move forward with my life and continue walking along the path God designed for me. Everyone is not meant to take the journey with you. As much as it hurt me, and I could not understand God's plan, it was all in the making years before the breaking point. Although, at the time, I could not understand it or even fathom what was happening with me and my friendships, God was planning something magnificent with my life. God needed to use me as a vessel to continue His work on a larger scale.

Once I dedicated my life to Christ, I had immense blessings that I could not imagine would come to fruition. I could not imagine until I knew my purpose was to be a servant leader amongst God's people. When I committed to Christ, I knew God had bigger plans for me. I asked God to use me as a vessel to do His work.

I used my education to escape poverty and began creating a **legacy** for my family.

What is your purpose? Ask yourself, *is something holding me back from living in my purpose?*

Your blessings are waiting for you. Go get them.

Scripture

"Blessed be the Lord my strength, which teacheth my hands to war, and my fingers to fight." ~ Psalm 144:1

"Ye shall not fear them: For the Lord your God he shall fight for you." ~ Deuteronomy 3:22

"The Lord shall fight for you, and ye shall hold your peace." ~ Exodus 14:14

"For my yoke is easy, and my burden is light." ~ Matthew 11:30

Songs of Inspiration

"Won't He Do It" ~ Koryn Hawthorne

"Go Get It" ~ Mary Mary

Scripture Summary

"What the devil meant for harm, God
meant for Good." ~ Genesis 50:20

"The Lord shall fight for you, and ye shall
hold your peace." ~ Exodus 14:14

"Ye shall not fear them: For the Lord your God
he shall fight for you." ~ Deuteronomy 3:22

"Acquaint now thyself with him and be at peace:
thereby good shall come unto thee." ~ Job 22:21-22

"Thou shalt make thy prayer unto him, and he shall
hear thee, and thy shall pay thou vows." ~ Job 27:30

"Lord, you know the hopes of the helpless. Surely you
will hear their cries and comfort them." ~ Psalm 10:17

"The LORD is my shepherd; I shall not want. ~ Psalm 23:1

"I waited patiently for the Lord; he turned to me
and heard my cry... He set my feet on a rock and
gave me a firm place to stand." ~ Psalm 40:1-2

"The Lord is on my side; I will not fear: what
can man do unto me?" ~ Psalm 118:6

"Blessed be the Lord my strength, which teacheth my
hands to war, and my fingers to fight" ~ Psalm 144:1

"Great is the Lord, and greatly to be praised, and
his greatness is unsearchable." ~ Psalm 145:3

"He healeth the broken in heart and bindeth
up their wounds." ~Psalm 147:3

"To everything there is a season and a time to every
purpose under the heaven."~ Ecclesiastes 3:1

"Fear thou not, for I am with thee: be not dismayed; for
I am thy God: I will strengthen thee." ~ Isaiah 41:10

"No weapon that is formed against thee shall prosper,
and every tongue that shall rise against thee in
judgment thou shalt condemn." ~ Isaiah 54:17

DR. FATIMA A. MCCOY-LEONARD

"I know the plans I have for you." ~ Jeremiah 29:11

"Let your light shine before men, that they may see your good works, and glorify your Father which is in heaven." ~ Matthew 5:16

"For if ye forgive men their trespasses, your heavenly Father will also forgive you." ~ Matthew 6:14

"Judge not, that ye be not judged. For with what judgment ye judge, ye shall be judged: and with what measure ye mete, it shall be measured to you again." ~ Matthew 7:1

"Ask, and it shall be given you; seek and ye shall find; knock, and it shall be opened unto you." ~ Matthew 7:7

"And blessed is he, whosoever shall not be offended in me." ~ Matthew 11:6

"For my yoke is easy, and my burden is light." ~ Matthew 11:30

"And all things, whatsoever ye shall ask in prayer, believing, ye shall receive." ~ Matthew 21:22

"The spirit is willing, but the flesh is weak." ~ Matthew 26:41

"Truly, I tell you. This very night, before the rooster crows twice, you will deny me three times." ~ Mark 14:72

"For with God nothing shall be impossible. ~Luke 1:37

"Although I want to do good, evil is right
there with me." ~ Romans 7:21

"Thanks be to God, who delivers me through
Jesus Christ our Lord!" ~ Romans 7:25

"If God be for us, who can be against us?" ~ Romans 8:31

"So then faith comes by hearing, and hearing
by the word of God." ~ Romans 10:17

"God can do exceedingly and abundantly above all
beyond what you can ask for." ~Ephesians 3:20-21

"I can do all things through Christ which
strengthens me." ~ Philippians 4:13

"Forbearing one another, and forgiving one another,
even as Christ forgave you." ~ Colossians 3:13

"Now faith is the substance of things hoped for, the
evidence of things not seen." ~Hebrews 11:1

Songs of Inspiration

***

"My Testimony" ~ Marvin Sapp

"You Don't Know" ~ Zacadi Cortez

"Gracefully Broken" ~ Tasha Cobbs-Leonard

"Great Is Your Mercy" ~ Donnie McClurkin

"We Gon' Be Alright" ~ Tye Tribbett

"In the Midst Of It All" ~ Yolanda Adams

"He Has His Hands On You" ~ Marvin Sapp

"You Deserve It" ~ JJ Hairston & Youthful Praise

"I Almost Let Go" ~ Kurt Carr

"Better Days" ~ Le'Andia Johnson

"Never Would Have Made It" ~ Marvin Sapp

"Change Me" ~ Tamela Mann

"Grateful" ~ Hezekiah Walker

"He's Intentional" ~ Travis Greene

"Be Blessed" ~ Yolanda Adams

"When I Pray" ~ Doe

"Hello Fear" ~ Kirk Franklin

"Break Every Chain" ~ Tamela Mann

"Let Go, Let God" ~ PJ Morton featuring The Walls Group

"He Turned It" ~ Tye Tribett

"God's Got A Blessing" ~ Norman Hutchins

"Wanna Be Happy" ~ Kirk Franklin

"Never Gave Up" ~ JJ Hairston, Travis Greene

"Something Has to Break" ~ Tasha Cobbs-Leonard

"Won't He Do It" ~ Koryn Hawthorne

"Go Get It" ~ Mary Mary

Reference

Frothingham, M. B., Simply Psychology. *Imposter Syndrome: Definition, Symptoms, Types, And Coping* Retrieved from https://www.simplypsychology.org/imposter-syndrome.html

STAY CONNECTED WITH
FATIMA MCCOY-LEONARD, Ed.D.

www.ingramcontent.com/pod-product-compliance
Lightning Source LLC
Chambersburg PA
CBHW060331130626
46553CB00003B/969